FROM:

THE
Wisdom
OF
Angels

COMPILED BY

JAX BERMAN

PETER PAUPER PRESS, INC.
WHITE PLAINS, NEW YORK

Designed by Margaret Rubiano

Illustrations © Shutterstock.com

Copyright © 2020
Peter Pauper Press, Inc.
202 Mamaroneck Avenue
White Plains, NY 10601 USA
ISBN 978-1-4413-3214-1
Printed in China

7 6 5 4 3 2 1

Visit us at www.peterpauper.com

THE
Wisdom
OF
Angels

*a*ngels walk among us, although not all of them have wings. They look like us, they sound like us . . . well, actually, they *are* us. Angelic messengers, spirit guides, the universe, your higher power—whatever you choose to call them—inspire flashes of insight or guidance if we listen and trust. Everyday people and unsung heroes do great things in the name of good, whether it's giving back to the entire community or being there for just one person. And so do we.

This little book inspires us to notice the still, small voice within, and to be a warrior for love as we manifest a spark of the Divine in our world. Within these pages, you'll find quotes from thinkers, philosophers, writers, and more, detailing what it really means to be an angel—to be compassionate, kind, and a source of light for those around you. Let these words remind you to throw kindness around like confetti!

WE ARE NOT
human beings
having a spiritual
experience.
WE ARE
spiritual beings
having a human
experience.

PIERRE TEILHARD DE CHARDIN

Hope is like compassion to me. It's like possibility and living in possibility.

MORLEY

Kind words

ARE THE MUSIC OF THE
WORLD. THEY HAVE A POWER
WHICH SEEMS TO BE BEYOND
NATURAL CAUSES, AS IF THEY
WERE SOME ANGEL'S SONG
WHICH HAD LOST ITS WAY AND
come on earth.

FREDERICK WILLIAM FABER

YOU ARE A CHILD
OF THE UNIVERSE
NO LESS THAN THE
TREES AND THE
STARS; YOU HAVE
a right to be here.
AND WHETHER OR
NOT IT IS CLEAR TO
YOU, NO DOUBT
THE UNIVERSE IS
unfolding as it should.

MAX EHRMANN, *DESIDERATA*

All God's angels come to us disguised.

JAMES RUSSELL LOWELL

As the human race, let's continue to *show love,* compassion, and respect toward one another.

Amber J. Liu

It's amazing what *miracles and little angels* AND PURE LOVE AROUND YOU CAN BRING OUT.

TIONNE WATKINS

We shall find *peace.* WE SHALL HEAR THE ANGELS, WE SHALL SEE THE SKY *sparkling with diamonds.*

ANTON CHEKHOV

For truly we are
all angels
temporarily
hiding as humans.

BRIAN L. WEISS

COMPASSION IS A CALL,
a demand of nature,
TO RELIEVE THE
UNHAPPY; AS HUNGER
IS A NATURAL CALL
for food.

JOSEPH BUTLER

MANY PEOPLE THINK
angels are only
THERE FOR THE BIG
EVENTS, OR WHEN WE
SUMMON THEM IN
PRAYER. THE TRUTH IS,
OUR ANGELS STAND
beside us always.

TRUDY GRISWOLD AND BARBARA MARK

A SELFISH PERSON CONDEMNS HIMSELF TO DREADFUL LONELINESS AND COMPLETE OBLIVION.

Happiness is in giving love, AND HAPPIER IS THE ONE WHO LOVES RATHER THAN THE ONE WHO IS LOVED. WHEN THIS TRUTH IS REALIZED, ALL HAPPINESS WILL MATERIALIZE.

HELENA ROERICH

I've got angels watching out for me.

ISAAC HANSON

Yes, Love indeed is *light* from *heaven*;
A spark of that immortal *fire*
With *angels* shared, by Allah given,
To *lift* from earth our low *desire*.

LORD BYRON

We are each of us
angels with only
one wing,
AND WE CAN ONLY FLY
by embracing
one another.

LUCIANO DE CRESCENZO

As I get older, the more I stay *focused* on the acceptance of myself and others, and choose *compassion* over judgment, and *curiosity* over fear.

TRACEE ELLIS

Angels encourage us by guiding us onto a path that will lead to *happiness* and *hope.*

ANDY LAKEY

Butterflies hover
and feathers
APPEAR WHENEVER
lost loved ones
or angels
ARE NEAR.

We are all angelic.
Offspring of godly relic,
accept and
be prophetic.

GLORIA D. GONSALVES

I THINK WE NEED MORE *love in the world.* WE NEED MORE KINDNESS, MORE COMPASSION, MORE JOY, MORE LAUGHTER. I DEFINITELY WANT TO *contribute to that.*

ELLEN DeGENERES

May the *light of peace* comfort you. May the presence of angels soothe you. May the *spirit of love* heal you. You are safe, protected.

STEFFANY BARTON

True compassion

MEANS NOT ONLY FEELING
ANOTHER'S PAIN BUT
ALSO BEING MOVED TO
help relieve it.

DANIEL GOLEMAN

GOD'S DREAM IS THAT
YOU AND I AND ALL OF
US WILL REALIZE THAT
we are family,
THAT WE ARE MADE FOR
togetherness,
FOR GOODNESS, AND
FOR COMPASSION.

DESMOND TUTU

Until he extends
HIS CIRCLE OF
compassion
to include all
living things,
MAN WILL NOT
himself find peace.

ALBERT SCHWEITZER

But the *greatest mistake* is in believing that we are "only human." We are human in expression but divine in creation and *limitless* in *potentiality*.

ERIC BUTTERWORTH

To love for the
*sake of being loved
is human,*
BUT TO LOVE FOR
*the sake of loving is
angelic.*

ALPHONSE DE LAMARTINE

ONE'S LIFE HAS *value* SO LONG AS ONE ATTRIBUTES VALUE TO THE LIFE OF OTHERS, BY MEANS OF *love, friendship, indignation, compassion.*

SIMONE DE BEAUVOIR

No act of
kindness, no
matter how
small, is ever
wasted.

Aesop

I HEARD AN ANGEL
singing
WHEN THE DAY WAS
springing,
"MERCY, PITY AND
peace
ARE THE WORLD'S
release."

WILLIAM BLAKE

Shall we make
a new rule of life
from tonight:
Always to try to be
a little kinder
than is necessary?

J. M. BARRIE

O passing *Angel*,
SPEED ME WITH
A SONG,
A *melody* OF HEAVEN
TO REACH MY HEART
AND ROUSE ME TO THE
RACE AND MAKE
ME *strong*.

CHRISTINA ROSSETTI

WHEN ANGELS
VISIT US, WE DO NOT
HEAR THE RUSTLE OF
wings, NOR FEEL THE
FEATHERY TOUCH OF
THE BREAST OF A DOVE;
BUT WE KNOW THEIR
presence BY THE
LOVE THEY CREATE IN
OUR *hearts.*

MARY BAKER EDDY

TOO OFTEN WE
UNDERESTIMATE THE
power OF A TOUCH,
A SMILE, A KIND WORD,
A LISTENING EAR, AN
honest COMPLIMENT,
OR THE SMALLEST ACT
OF CARING, ALL OF
WHICH HAVE THE
POTENTIAL TO TURN
A LIFE *around*.

LEO BUSCAGLIA

We must teach *compassion* and *tolerance* and encourage *kindness,* *selflessness,* and *loving* *acceptance* of all who are created in the image of God.

EPHRAIM MIRVIS

LIFE IS MADE UP, NOT
OF GREAT SACRIFICES
OR DUTIES, BUT OF
little things, IN
WHICH SMILES AND
KINDNESSES AND
SMALL OBLIGATIONS,
GIVEN HABITUALLY, ARE
WHAT WIN AND
preserve the heart,
AND SECURE COMFORT.

SIR HUMPHRY DAVY

Be an angel to
someone else
WHENEVER YOU CAN,
as a way of
thanking God
FOR THE HELP
your angel has
given you.

EILEEN ELIAS FREEMAN

CARE ABOUT
THE BEINGS YOU
CARE ABOUT IN
gorgeous AND
surprising WAYS.
COLOR OUTSIDE
THE LINES. PRACTICE
RANDOM KINDNESS
AND SENSELESS
ACTS OF *beauty.*

ANNE HERBERT

But whoever has the *world's goods,* and sees his brother in need, and closes his heart of compassion against him, how does the love of God remain in him? My little children, let's not love in word only, or with the tongue only, *but in deed and truth.*

1 John 3:17–18, *World English Bible*

The highest forms of understanding WE CAN ACHIEVE are laughter and human compassion.

RICHARD FEYNMAN

Men are only *great* as they are *kind.*

ELBERT HUBBARD

Compassion IN THE HIGHEST DEGREE IS THE *divinest* FORM OF RELIGION.

ALICE MEYNELL

I could see their
woe and sadness
And I pledged
to ease their pain
Their suff'ring
would not be
in vain

THE PRINCE, FROM *THE PRINCE AND THE PAUPER*

WHAT A PIECE OF
WORK IS A MAN! HOW
NOBLE IN *reason*, HOW
INFINITE IN FACULTY!
IN FORM AND MOVING
HOW EXPRESS AND
ADMIRABLE! IN ACTION
HOW LIKE AN *angel*, IN
APPREHENSION HOW
LIKE A GOD!

WILLIAM SHAKESPEARE

If we can share our story with someone who responds with empathy and understanding, shame can't survive.

BRENÉ BROWN

Happiness AND *peace*
WILL COME TO EARTH
ONLY AS THE *light*
OF *love* AND HUMAN
COMPASSION ENTER
THE SOULS OF MEN.

David O. McKay

WOULDN'T IT BE WONDERFUL
IF WE COULD ALL BE A LITTLE
MORE *gentle* WITH EACH
OTHER, AND A LITTLE MORE
loving, HAVE A LITTLE
MORE *empathy*, AND
MAYBE WE'D LIKE EACH
OTHER A LITTLE BIT MORE.

JUDY GARLAND

For he will put his angels in charge of you, to guard you IN ALL YOUR WAYS. They will bear you UP IN THEIR HANDS, so that you won't dash your foot against a stone.

Psalm 91:11–12, World English Bible

IT IS NOT BECAUSE
ANGELS ARE *holier*
THAN MEN OR DEVILS
THAT MAKES THEM
angels, BUT BECAUSE
THEY DO NOT EXPECT
holiness FROM ONE
ANOTHER, BUT FROM
GOD ALONE.

WILLIAM BLAKE

Angels are all around us, all the time, in the very air we breathe.

Eileen Elias Freeman

A THOUGHT TRANSFIXED ME:
FOR THE FIRST TIME IN MY
LIFE I SAW THE *truth* AS
IT IS SET INTO SONG BY SO
MANY POETS, PROCLAIMED AS
THE *final wisdom* BY SO
MANY THINKERS.
THE TRUTH—THAT LOVE
IS THE ULTIMATE AND THE
highest goal TO WHICH
MAN CAN ASPIRE.

VIKTOR FRANKL

When hours are filled with *sadness* and you need someone to *care*, it's so helpful to remember that angels are *aware*.

Author unknown

A gentle word,
a kind look,
a good-natured
smile can work
wonders and
accomplish
miracles.

WILLIAM HAZLITT

Sweet souls AROUND
US! WATCH US STILL,
PRESS NEARER TO
OUR SIDE,
INTO *our thoughts,*
INTO OUR PRAYERS,
WITH GENTLE
helpings GLIDE.

HARRIET BEECHER STOWE

You are not here *merely* to prepare to make a living. You are here in order to enable the world to live more *amply*, with greater vision, with a finer spirit of *hope* and *achievement*. You are here to enrich the world, and you impoverish yourself if you *forget* the errand.

Woodrow Wilson

What makes us different from other species is our capacity for compassion and empathy with the struggles of other people.

LIAM CUNNINGHAM

HAVING A VESTED INTEREST IN OTHER SOULS *unconditionally* CREATES A RIPPLE EFFECT THAT PRODUCES *miracles* IN THE LIVES OF THOSE AROUND US.

MOLLY FRIEDENFELD

I THINK WE ALL DO HAVE A GUARDIAN ANGEL. I BELIEVE THEY WORK *through* US ALL THE TIME, WHEN WE ARE *thoughtful* AND *good* AND *kind* TO EACH OTHER.

ROMA DOWNEY

CARRY OUT A *random* ACT OF KINDNESS, WITH *no expectation* OF REWARD, SAFE IN THE KNOWLEDGE THAT ONE DAY *someone* MIGHT DO THE SAME FOR YOU.

PRINCESS DIANA

I GO MY WAY, AND MY LEFT FOOT SAYS *"Glory,"* AND MY RIGHT FOOT SAYS *"Amen"*: IN AND OUT OF SHADOW CREEK, UPSTREAM AND DOWN, *exultant,* IN A DAZE, DANCING, TO THE TWIN SILVER TRUMPETS *of praise.*

ANNIE DILLARD

Love can defeat
that nameless terror.
Loving one another,
we take the sting
from death.

EDWARD ABBEY

May *wings of light*
GUIDE YOU.
I DO NOT AT ALL
UNDERSTAND THE
MYSTERY OF *grace* —
ONLY THAT IT MEETS
US WHERE WE ARE BUT
DOES NOT LEAVE US
WHERE IT FOUND US.

ANNE LAMOTT

*Angels have
no philosophy
but love.*

TERRI GUILLEMETS

We have to *fill our hearts* WITH GRATITUDE. *Gratitude* MAKES EVERYTHING THAT WE HAVE *more* THAN ENOUGH.

SUSAN L. TAYLOR

ANGELS LIVE AMONG
US. SOMETIMES THEY
hide their wings,
BUT THERE IS
NO DISGUISING
THE PEACE AND
hope they bring.

AUTHOR UNKNOWN

Love allows
a person to see
the true
angelic nature
of another person,
the halo, the aureole
of divinity.

THOMAS MOORE

Angels are not beings with wings; they are feelings that give us wings.

INA CATRINESCU

*May angels surround
you, guide you, and
walk beside you.*